Sharks have been around for a very long time. They can be big or small and they come in lots of different shapes. Many sharks are shy and harmless. Only a few sharks will attack a person.

The body of a shark is smooth and long. Sharks have strong tails that help them swim quickly.

denticles

Their skin has thousands of little scales. These scales are called denticles and they all point to the tail of the shark. They will rip anything that rubs up against them.

Sharks have lots of teeth. The teeth are different shapes, according to the job they have to do. Some are sharp and pointed and some are flat for crushing things. Sharks have several lines of teeth. If a tooth falls out, another one fills the gap!

teeth

The fin on the back of a shark is called the dorsal fin. It is this fin that you think of, sticking up out of the sea, when you think of a shark.

dorsal fin

Sharks do sometimes attack surfers and swimmers. This could be because the sharks think they look like the seals and turtles they normally eat. Look at the shape of a surfer, a seal and a turtle from underneath.

One of the biggest fish in the sea today is a shark: the whale shark. It can grow to 12m long. A whale shark does not have any teeth. Instead, it has filters to catch plankton. It swims along with its mouth wide, and the plankton float in and are trapped.

whale shark

remoras

There are often black and white striped fish swimming by the whale shark's mouth. These are called remoras and they help the whale shark by eating small animals off the body of the shark.

Sharks have very good senses. They can smell food from a long way away. They have sensors on their snouts that pick up electrical signals that other fish and animals send out.

hammerhead

The hammerhead shark has a very oddly shaped head. No one knows exactly why the hammerhead has this shaped head. It swings its head from side to side to sense the things around it.

Sharks have to keep swimming, or they sink...

...so they have to swim all the time, even when they are asleep!

The biggest shark that ever lived was called megalodon. It lived a very, very long time ago. No one knows exactly how big a megalodon was, but it would have been enormous.

megalodon

Some sharks, like the dogfish, lay eggs. The outside case of the egg is leathery. The case attaches itself to seaweed by twisted strands, until the egg hatches.

mermaid's purse

You often see them lying on the beach. Sometimes they are called mermaid's purses.

thresher

The thresher shark has a very long, curved tail. The tail is as long as the head and the body together. It flicks its tail from side to side as it swims around a shoal of fish. The fish end up in a tight ball, which makes it easier for the shark to catch them.

The wobbegong belongs to the shark family. It has frilly bits of skin hanging across its mouth. It lies in wait on the bottom of the sea and when animals and fish investigate the frill, the wobbegong snaps them up.

wobbegong

It is difficult to see it on the bottom because of the pattern on its skin.

Rays belong to the same family as sharks. They are flat fish with wings, which they flap as they swim along.

stingray

The stingray is so called because it has a poisonous spine or "sting" on its tail. Hammerhead sharks hunt stingrays. The poison in the stingray's tail does not affect the sharks.

Man is the shark's biggest enemy. Some beaches have nets put around them to keep sharks out. Lots of sharks are killed in the nets. The sharks get tangled in the nets and drown, as they cannot swim. Men kill many more sharks than sharks kill men.

Reading Comprehension

Teachers and parents

An important part of becoming a confident, fluent reader is a child's ability to understand what they are reading. Below are some suggestions on how to develop a child's reading comprehension.

- Make reading this book a shared experience between you and the child. Try to avoid leaving it until the whole book is read before talking about it. Occasionally stop at various intervals throughout the book.
- Ask questions about the characters, the setting, the action and the meaning.
- Encourage the child to think about what might happen next. It does not matter if the answer is right or wrong, so long as the suggestion makes sense and demonstrates understanding.
- Ask the child to describe what is happening in the illustrations.
- Relate what is happening in the book to any real-life experiences the child may have.
- Pick out any vocabulary that may be new to the child and ask what they think it means. If they don't know, explain it and relate it to what is happening in the book.
- Encourage the child to summarise, in their own words, what they have read.

What's in the book?

- What happens if a shark loses a tooth?
- What length can a whale shark grow to?
- What happens if a shark stops swimming?

What do you think?

- Why is the hammerhead shark called by that name?
- Why are some people frightened of sharks?

Jolly Phonics Readers
are fully decodable books for new readers

These readers have been written with a **carefully controlled vocabulary,** and are specifically designed for children who are learning to read and write with Jolly Phonics.

- The text in these Blue Level Books (fourth level) uses only **decodable regular words** that use the letter-sound knowledge taught so far: the 42 main letter sounds, <y> as in *happy*, and the main alternative vowel spellings (the 'hop-over <e>' spellings of the long vowel sounds, <ay> as in *day*, <ea> as in *seat*, <y> and <igh> as in *fly* and *high*, <ow> as in *low* and *now*, <ew> as in *dew*, <oy> as in *joy*, <ir> and <ur> as in *bird* and *turn*, and <al>, <au> and <aw> as in *talk*, *pause* and *saw*), and a small number of **tricky words** (frequently used words that are not fully decodable at this stage).

- All new tricky words and alternative vowel spellings used are shown on the front inside cover. These can be used as a quick practice activity before starting the book.

- **Faint type** is used for silent letters, like the <b> in *lamb*.

- **Comprehension questions** and discussion topics are included at the end of the book. These ensure that children are not only able to read the text, but also get meaning from it.

Blue Level Readers

Level 0 Level 1   Level 4

Inky Mouse & Friends
The Bird House
Daisy and Buttercup
The New Kitten
An Inter-Hive Match
The Maize Maze
Beach Rescue

General Fiction
The Enormous Turnip
Rumpelstiltskin
Puppets
Many More Monsters
The Pumpkin Party
Town Mouse and Country Mouse

Nonfiction
Soccer
Mountains
Henry Ford
Sharks
The Moon
The Nile

To see the full range of Jolly Phonics products, visit our website at www.jollylearning.co.uk

© Sara Wernham 2007 (text) © Kevin Maddison 2007 (illustrations)

77 Hornbeam Road, Buckhurst Hill, Essex, IG9 6JX, UK
Tel: +44 20 8501 0405

82 Winter Sport Lane, Williston, VT 05495, USA
Tel: +1-800-488-2665

Printed in China. All rights reserved.
www.jollylearning.co.uk
info@jollylearning.co.uk

100% Paper from well-managed forests
FSC® C146541

ISBN 978-1-84414-065-7

Reference: JL652

Nonfiction

The Moon

Jolly Phonics

Teachers and parents

Before tackling these Blue Level Readers, a child will need to be able to:
- Recognise the basic 42 letter sounds, ‹y› as in *happy*, the 'hop-over ‹e›' digraphs in words like *take, these, bike, code* and *mule,* and the other main alternative vowel spellings in the leaves below;
- Read (blend) regular words containing these letter sounds;
- Recognise the twenty tricky words shown in the flowers below;
- Recognise the names of the three main characters, as well as Phonic.

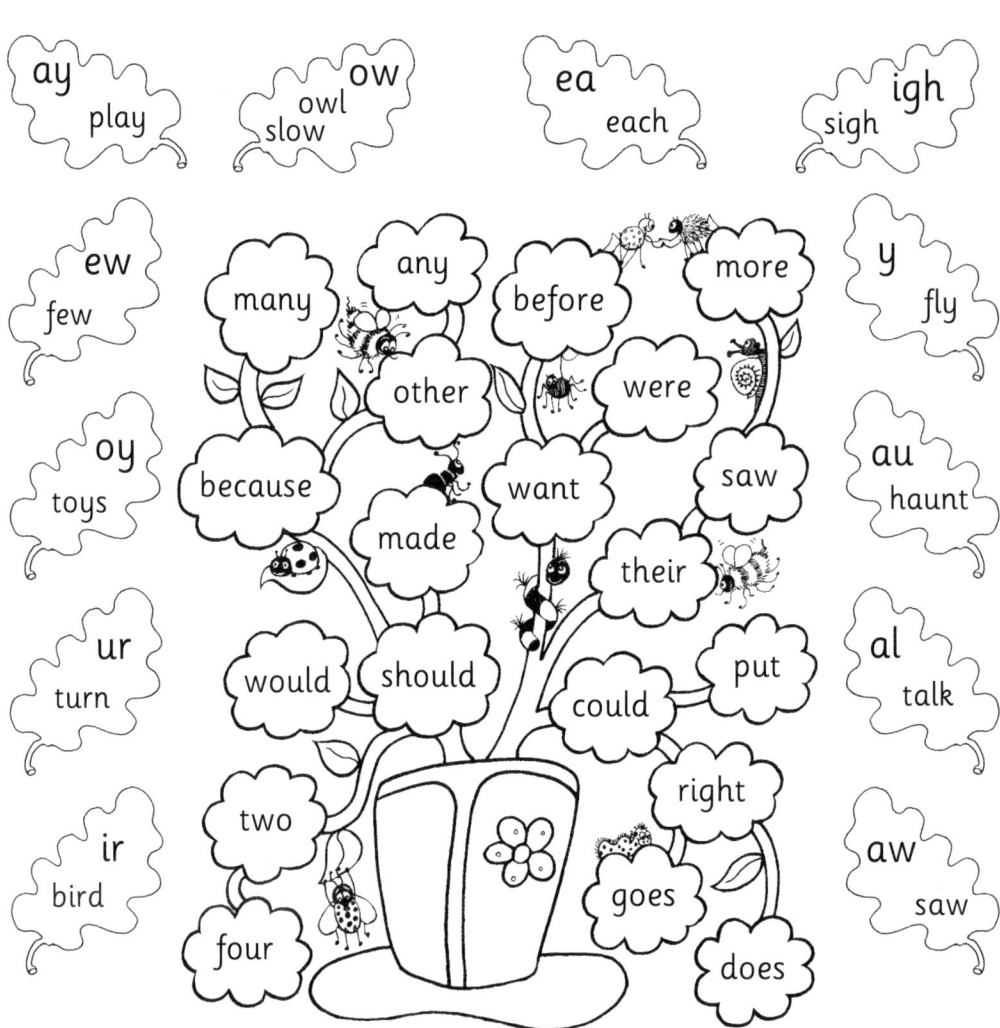